AF595900

NYUNTU NINTI

(What you should know)

For our family,
our land,
our home.

Kanyini is a sacred principle of unconditional love and responsibility to all things.
It is a principle that underpins Aboriginal life, linking four main areas of responsibility:
Tjukurrpa (philosophy, law and religion), Ngura (home and country),
Waltyja (family and kinship) and Kurunpa (spirit, soul and psyche).
As humans, we have to connect to and be responsible for each one of these areas.

Nyuntu Ninti means 'what you should know'.

NYUNTU NINTI

(What you should know)

Bob Randall and Melanie Hogan

My name is Bob Randall and I'm an Aṉangu man from Uluṟu.

Uluṟu is the largest rock in the world. When I see her,
I feel as though I'm home.

I belong here.

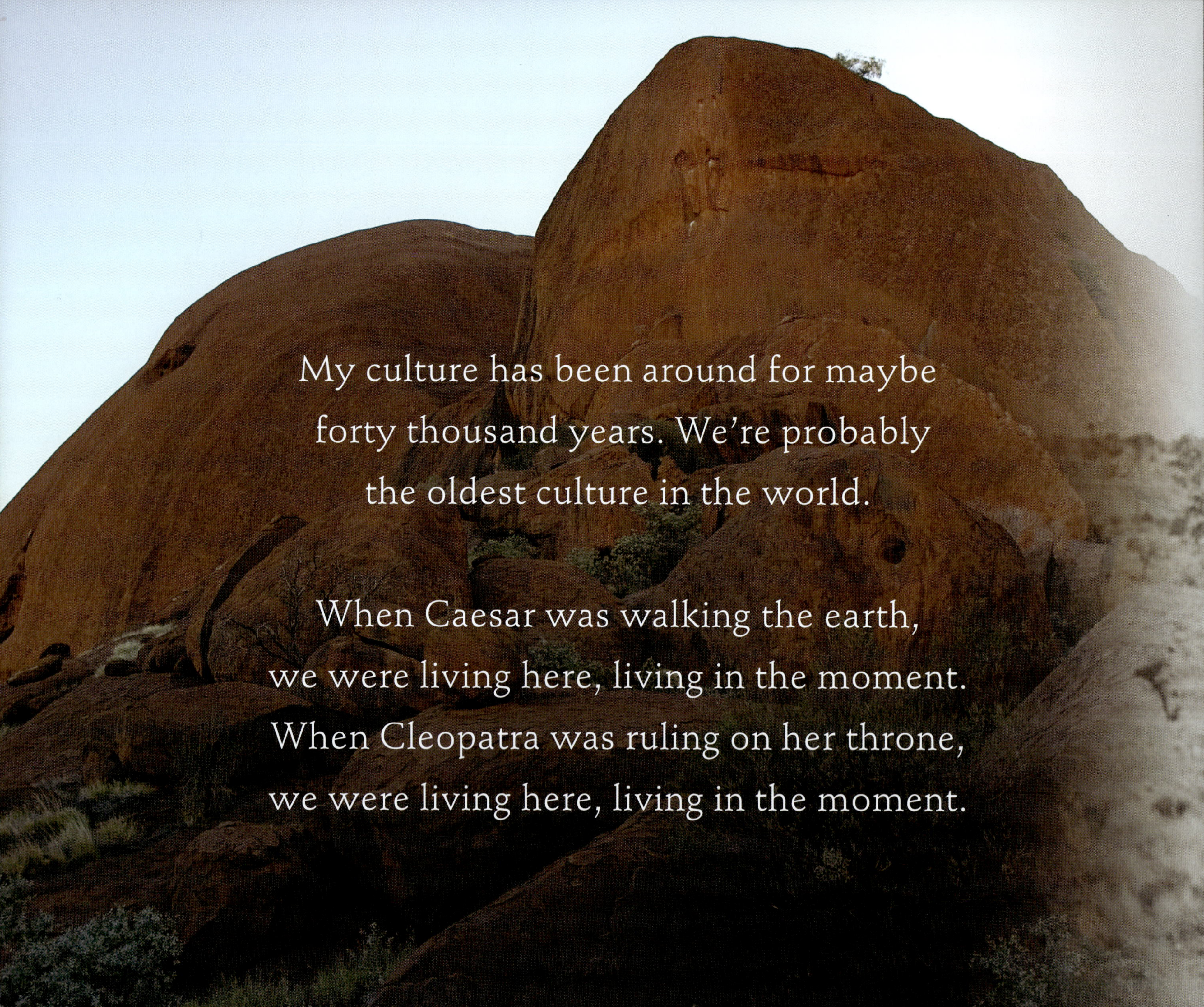

My culture has been around for maybe
forty thousand years. We're probably
the oldest culture in the world.

When Caesar was walking the earth,
we were living here, living in the moment.
When Cleopatra was ruling on her throne,
we were living here, living in the moment.

For thousands of years, these things you think ancient, we were living here, living in the moment.

Now we share this country with many different cultures, but I can still feel my ancestors who have walked on this earth before me.

Not many people know much about us.
That's why I want to share some things with you.
Things about us. About our land.
Things you may not have heard before.

Us mob, we're from the desert.
It's really hot where we come from.
Really hot and really beautiful.

Everything here is my family. It's all bush as far as you can see, but to me, it is my home, my ngura. The trees are our family, all the animals that live with us are our family.

Growing up with the oldies — our parents, grandparents — they always said we are connected to everything.

Being alive connects you to every other
living thing that's around you.
You're never lost and you're never, ever alone —
you're one with everything else that there is.

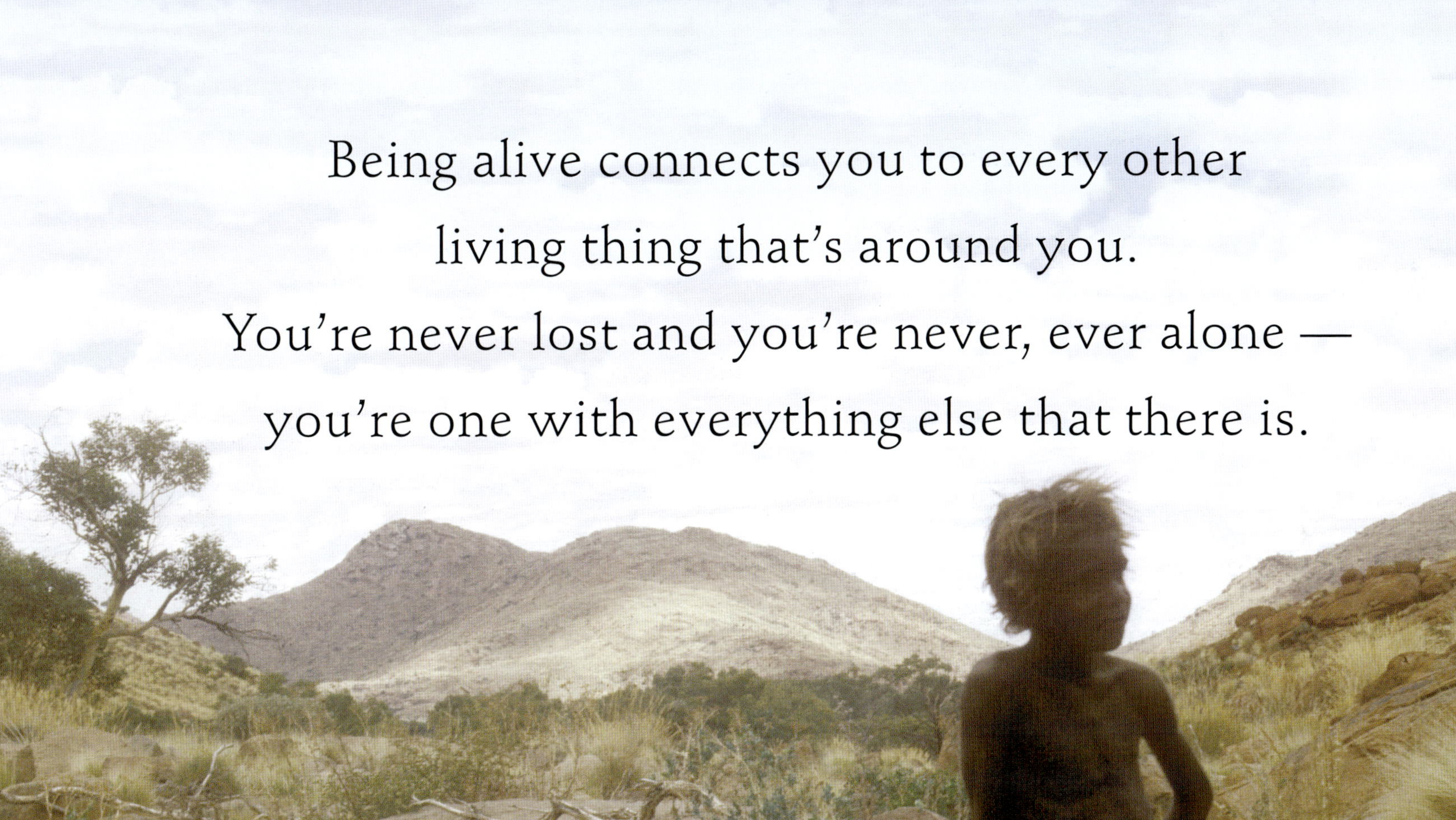

The purpose of life is to
be part of all that there is.

Living in the bush we are communicating with everything — the wind, the trees, the flowers, the grass. Every action is an action of beauty. We are aware of everything that is around us. It's that connection to the land that makes you feel so good.

Where we came from

Words by Bob Randall

Chorus

You know the sun and the moon
and the stars up in the sky.
You see the mountains
and the flowers and the trees.
You see the river and the sea,
feel the wind that blows the breeze,
that is where and from them all,
you come from.

Late at night, just after tea,
my baby boy came up to me.
With his eyes shining bright,
he said to me, Daddy, I want to know
about some things that bother me.
Daddy, where did I come from?

Chorus

Well, my son, all I can say
are the things once said to me
by your grandpa and your grandma, so long ago.
In the past when things were men
and men were things, long, long ago,
these are the words that, when I asked,
were said to me.

Chorus

Our ancestors in the past
walked this land and made the Law,
saying all living things are all the same.
We may be different in many ways,
but we should live in harmony
with all things and each other all our days.

Chorus

My people have always been part of the earth.
Every single inch of this land
and its waterways is sacred land.

I was born in the bush, I was a bush baby.
I had no clothes, my parents had no clothes.
We all walked around in our natural state, same as
the trees, same as the kangaroo and the emu.

The earth is our mother.
We are born from her.
She looks after us with meat,
bush tucker and water.

We used to walk right
throughout this country.
As children our mothers
would walk with us and feed us,
give us water, nourish us,
and at night make the
shelters for us to sleep in.

We always slept on Mother Earth.

As we walked over country,
we didn't worry about building houses.
You don't need a house when you're alive.
You can move and you can leave it behind.

What I remember most about those times is that I was totally free. The choices were always mine, as it was with all the members of my family.

Our life was very disciplined. We were trained to look after the ceremonies, the land and each other. That was important to our people.

We didn't take more than we needed. We didn't destroy anything that could not produce again. We believe Mother Earth looks after us and we in turn must look after her.

Everything is ours. Everything is family.
No one is without when you think and live that way.

Sometimes I wish all the people in the world
could know this. Then more people would smile.

My people still live beside Uluṟu.

In my homeland, Indigenous and non-Indigenous people still seem confused about each other. We are finding it difficult to journey together. Knowing this, Uncle Bob and I wanted to create a film (*Kanyini*) that helps to bring Indigenous and non-Indigenous people closer together — not just in Australia, but all over the world. *Nyuntu Ninti* is based on *Kanyini*.

As a young person, I feel very strongly that many of the values held by our Indigenous brothers and sisters could be of enormous benefit for society at large; particularly their care and respect for Mother Earth and all forms of life. In a world that is going a little too fast, Indigenous wisdom may hold some of the answers non-Indigenous people are looking for.

Hearing Uncle Bob tell his people's heartbreaking story with such honesty and love, gentleness and strength continues to amaze me. Uncle Bob always says the hardest thing to change in the world is 'negative attitude'. If *Kanyini* and *Nyuntu Ninti* can help create some positive attitude, then we're on our way to healing some of the mistakes of the past. And that excites me.

I want to thank Uncle Bob for trusting me with his story. It's been an incredible journey — one that has only just begun.

Melanie Hogan

Purkarari! Nyangangka book munu wangka aṉangu wiyaringkuntja tjuṯa ngaṟanyi.

Be careful! This book contains pictures and voices of Pitjantjatjara and Yankunytjatjara people who have passed away.

The ABC 'Wave' device and the 'ABC KIDS' device are trademarks of the Australian Broadcasting Corporation and are used under licence by HarperCollins*Publishers* Australia.

HarperCollins*Publishers*
Australia • Brazil • Canada • France • Germany • Holland • India
Italy • Japan • Mexico • New Zealand • Poland • Spain • Sweden
Switzerland • United Kingdom • United States of America

HarperCollins acknowledges the Traditional Custodians of the land upon which we live and work, and pays respect to Elders past and present.

Published in paperback in 2011 by HarperCollins*Children'sBooks*
a division of HarperCollins*Publishers* Australia Pty Limited
ABN 36 009 913 517
harpercollins.com.au

Copyright © Bob Randall and Melanie Hogan 2008

The rights of Bob Randall and Melanie Hogan to identified as the authors of this work has been asserted by them in accordance with the *Copyright Amendment (Moral Rights) Act 2000.*

All rights reserved. No part may be reproduced, copied, scanned, stored in a retrieval system, recorded, or transmitted, in any form or by any means, without the prior written permission of the publisher.

A CIP Record is available from the National Library of Australia

ISBN 978 0 7333 2850 3

Cover and page. 3: Uluru © Mark Gowing 2008; boy on rock courtesy of Ara Irititja, p48722, Rhoda Jenkin Collection, Alalka, 12/1969; Serpent Dreaming by Barney Daniels © Corbis. Back cover, pages 1 and 2: Uluru © Mark Gowing 2008. Page 4: Bob Randall © Kia Mistillis 2008. Page 5: Uluru © Mark Gowing 2008. Page 6: rocks © Mark Gowing 2008. Page 7: Aboriginal man carrying child on shoulder courtesy of the SLSA, JRB Love Collection, PRG 214/45/B98, ca. 1937. Page 8: landscape courtesy of Ara Irititja, p14380, Bill Edwards Collection, phot. Bill Edwards, Victory Well, Everard Ranges, 10/1979. Page 9: woman carrying water, Mount Conner courtesy of the SLSA, Mountford Sheard Collection, 1302B, 1940. Page 10: Aboriginal man of the Musgrave Ranges courtesy of the SLSA, Mountford Sheard Collection, 1127YT, 1940. Page 11: Serpent Dreaming by Barney Daniels © Corbis. Page 12: flowers in the desert courtesy of Ara Irititja, p14454, Bill Edwards Collection, phot. Bill Edwards, (near) Amata, 1979. Page 13: children and adult female courtesy of Ara Irititja, p5108, David Trudinger Collection, phot. David Trudinger, Ernabella, 3/1940; landscape courtesy of Ara Irititja, p14113, Bill Edwards Collection, phot. Bill Edwards, Mann Ranges (area), 11/1978; lizard in hand courtesy of Ara Irititja, p6405, Shirley Gudgeon (Hill) Collection, phot. Shirley Gudgeon (Hill), James Ranges, 9/1962. Page 14: man sitting by well courtesy of Ara Irititja, p13912, Bill Edwards Collection, phot. Bill Edwards, Alkanyunta, 7/1976. Page 15: boy on rock courtesy of Ara Irititja, p48722, Rhoda Jenkin Collection, Alalka, 12/1969. Page 16: enjoying the water courtesy of Ara Irititja, p25947, Allan Pound Collection, phot. Allan Pound, Ernabella, 1/1939. Page 17: landscape courtesy of Ara Irititja, p7387, Fay Blackman Collection, phot. Fay Blackman, Aliwanyuwanyu, 1968. Page 18: two children and adult male by a tree courtesy of Ara Irititja, p15519, Frank & Mary Bennett Collection, phot. Frank & Mary Bennett, Ernabella (range), 1949. Page 19: Bob Randall with witchetty grub/honey ants on branch/honey ants on hand © Kia Mistillis 2008; landscape courtesy of Ara Irititja, p14037, Bill Edwards Collection, phot. Bill Edwards, (near) Aliwanyuwanyu, 9/1978. Page 20: Aboriginal woman holding child courtesy of the SLSA, JRB Love Collection, PRG 214/45/H4, ca. 1937; landscape courtesy of Ara Irititja, p4037, Alice Peucker (Job) Collection, phot. Alice Peucker (Job), (near) Ernabella, 9/1963. Page 21: people walking courtesy of Ara Irititja, p25933, Allan Pound Collection, phot. Allan Pound, Ernabella, 12/1938 – 1/1939. Page 22: man climbing tree courtesy of Ara Irititja, p5592, Len Young Family Collection, phot. JRB Love, Ernabella, 1937c. Page 23: children swinging from tree courtesy of Ara Irititja, p6149, Shirley Gudgeon (Hill) Collection, phot. Shirley Gudgeon (Hill), Ernabella, 1960. Page 24: group of Aboriginal men with children courtesy of the SLSA, JRB Love Collection, PRG 214/45/B96, ca. 1937. Page 25: landscape © Mark Gowing 2008. Page 26: child swinging from tree courtesy of Ara Irititja, p6150, Shirley Gudgeon (Hill) Collection, phot. Shirley Gudgeon (Hill), Ernabella, 1960. Page 27: children outside grass hut courtesy of Ara Irititja, p5277, Frank Halls Collection, phot. Frank Halls, Ernabella, 1948. Page 28: children in bushes courtesy of Ara Irititja, p6254, Shirley Gudgeon (Hill) Collection, phot. Shirley Gudgeon (Hill), Ernabella, 1961. Page 29: boys in cave courtesy of Ara Irititja, p9163, Bert Qualmann Collection, phot. Barbara Ridley, Alkanyunta, 1975. Page 30: rock © Mark Gowing 2008. Page 31 Bob Randall and Melanie Hogan © Chris Pavlich. Page 32: © Mark Gowing 2008.

Design and digital imaging by Ellie Exarchos
Typeset in 22/37 Stempel Garamond by Ellie Exarchos
Colour reproduction by Graphic Print Group, Adelaide
Printed in China by RR Donnelley

11 24